AWS

VIRTUAL PRIVATE CLOUD

LEARN THE VARIOUS ASPECTS OF AMAZON
VIRTUAL PRIVATE CLOUD (VPC)

ADNEY AINSLEY

i

Table of Contents

Amazon AWS VPC Introduction and Features   1

AWS VPC Tutorial – Introduction to Concepts   5

AWS VPC subnets   9

AWS VPC Elastic IP and NAT   24

Amazon S3 Bucket   33

Create AWS EC2 instance using CLI   40

Amazon Elastic Cloud Compute – Create Instance   49

EC2 Launch Instance page   49

Select the Amazon Machine Image (AMI)   50

Choose an instance type   52

Configure Instance details   53

Add Block Storage   55

Tag Instance   55

Configure Security Group   56

Review Instance launch   57

Key pair   58

Login to the server   59

Amazon Elastic Cloud Compute (EC2) – Introduction 62

Mount Amazon Elastic File System (EFS) to EC2   65

Steps to mount EFS on EC2   66

Launch AWS EC2 Server and Set Up Ubuntu   76

Virtual Private Cloud (VPC) Best Configuration
Practices   92

Amazon AWS VPC Introduction and Features

In this AWS VPC tutorial, we will see an introduction to AWS VPC. We will also look at some of the key features of Amazon VPC.

What is AWS VPC?

AWS VPC or Virtual Private Cloud is an Amazon service that allows you to create you own virtual network inside Amazon cloud and to use this virtual network to launch amazon resources. You can think of a VPC as your own network of machines and databases that live completely inside Amazon's infrastructure but can be managed as if they were in your own data center. Here's a diagram of a how a typical VPC setup looks like

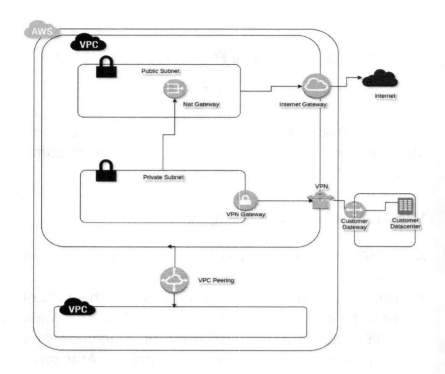

Features of AWS VPC

AWS VPC allows you to do the following. Not that this is not an exhaustive list, but highlights the important features:

- Create multiple Virtual networks (VPC) inside Amazon cloud.

- The VPC can span multiple regions and availability zones.
- Create multiple subnets within each VPC. Each subnet, however, can be in only one availability zone.
- The subnet can be private (not publicly accessible) or public (publicly accessible). The private subnet generally does not have public IP addresses.
- Manage access to the subnet using route tables and Access control list.
- Create Internet gateways to allow a subnet to be publically accessible.
- Add NAT gateways to allow a private subnet to access the internet.
- Create elastic IPs to attach to NAT gateways or other instances
- Allow connection between two VPC using VPC peering.
- Allow a secured private connection between a VPC and your own data center using a secured VPN connection. The secured connection as three parts:

   1. A VPN gateway in VPC
   2. The actual VPN connection

3. A customer gateway in the customer data center

This was just an introductory tutorial on Amazon VPC. In the next tutorial, we will look at how to create private and public subnets, add an internet gateway and add a NAT gateway.

AWS VPC Tutorial – Introduction to Concepts

In this AWS VPC tutorial, we will learn how to create a VPC; create public and private subnets that cover Multiple Availability zone; create CIDR blocks for each subnet; add Internet Gateways and NAT Gateways, and modify route table.

What is AWS VPC

Amazon VPC is your own private network inside Amazon's cloud infrastructure. It is an alternative to maintaining your own data centre and is cheaper since it creates resources on demand. It is also more secure since Amazon takes care of the infrastructure security for you.

What is a Subnet

We will not go into much detail about subnets from a networking point of view, but for this tutorial, you should know that subnet is a part of your VPC that can contain resources that share a common subnet mask and that contain instances and resources that can normally only be accessed within that subnet except if you use an internet gateway to make them public.

What is an Internet Gateway?

An Internet Gateway allows you to make a subnet public by providing a route to the internet. All instances within the subnet can access the internet only through this gateway. Also, resources from the internet can access the instances in your subnet using this gateway.

What is a NAT Gateway

You can allow instances from your private subnet to connect to the internet using a NAT gateway. The instances in the private subnet do not have an IP address, so the NAT gateway translates the private IP to a public IP before routing the traffic out to the internet. NAT stands for Network Address Translation and it does just that – translates private IPs to public IP.

What is a CIDR block

CIDR or Classless Inter-Domain Routing is used to allocate IP address within a network. We will use

CIDR blocks to mark a range of IP addresses for each subnet within a VPC. The VPC itself would have a CIDR block that lists all the IP addresses available with it.

What is a Route table

A route table contains rules for routing traffic within a subnet and from the subnet to outside world. Amongst other things, we use routing tables to add internet gateways and NAT gateways to the subnet.

Problem Statement for AWS VPC Tutorial

Here's the network that we are planning to build today. It has the following components:

1. A VPC spanning a region
2. Two public and two private subnets in two Availability Zones (AZ). (one AZ contains one public and one private network)
3. Internet Gateways for each public subnet in each AZ
   One NAT Gateway for each private subnet.

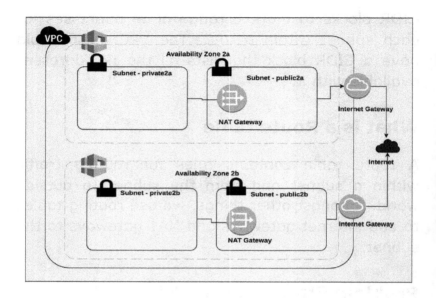

In the Next part, we will look at how to create the CIDR block for creating the subnets. We will also see how to create the VPC and the Subnets. In the third part we will see how to create internet gateways, NAT gateways and route tables.

AWS VPC subnets

In this AWS VPC tutorial, we will look at how to create the VPC, public and private subnets, route table, and an internet gateway.

AWS VPC Recap

In the previous tutorial we saw an introduction to Amazon VPC and also looked at the key concepts in VPC. Here's the diagram of what we are trying to accomplish

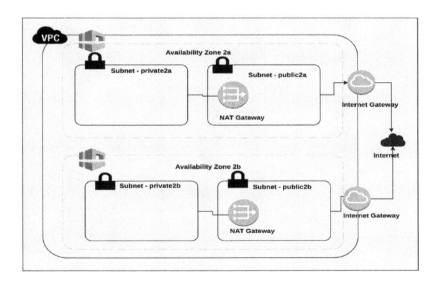

We begin by creating the VPC.

Creating VPC

We will look at how to create the VPC using the AWS management console. Login to the console and click on VPC. This is what you should see:

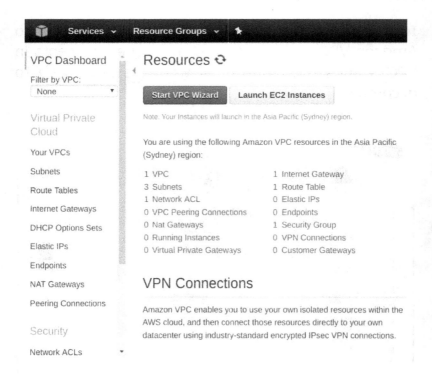

We will not be using the Wizard since we want to learn the inner workings of the VPC. Click on the link that says '1 VPC'. If you havent created a VPC before, you should still see 1 VPC which is the default that AWS creates for you. In the next screen you should see that one VPC and a button to 'Create VPC'

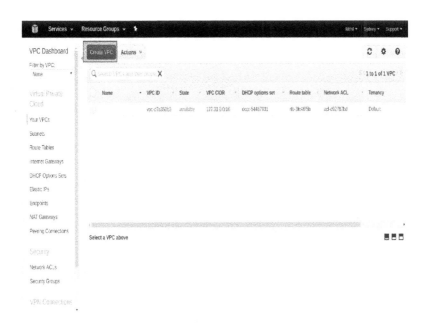

Creating CIDR block for VPC and Subnets

When you click 'Create VPC', you should see a popup where you can enter the VPC name and a CIDR block. This CIDR block determines the range of IP addresses that your VPC can have. It also specifies the network part of the IP addresses and the subnet mask. Here's how our VPC and the subnets in the VPC will look like.

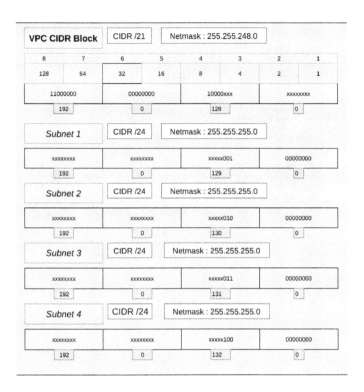

VPC CIDR Block	CIDR /21	Netmask : 255.255.248.0					
8	7	6	5	4	3	2	1
128	64	32	16	8	4	2	1
11000000		00000000		10000xxx		xxxxxxxx	
192		0		128		0	

Subnet 1	CIDR /24	Netmask : 255.255.255.0	
xxxxxxxx	xxxxxxxx	xxxxx001	00000000
192	0	129	0

Subnet 2	CIDR /24	Netmask : 255.255.255.0	
xxxxxxxx	xxxxxxxx	xxxxx010	00000000
192	0	130	0

Subnet 3	CIDR /24	Netmask : 255.255.255.0	
xxxxxxxx	xxxxxxxx	xxxxx011	00000000
192	0	131	0

Subnet 4	CIDR /24	Netmask : 255.255.255.0	
xxxxxxxx	xxxxxxxx	xxxxx100	00000000
192	0	132	0

CIDR block for the AWS VPC

We create a CIDR block keeping in mind the number of IP addresses that we want in our VPC. In this example, we have chosen a CIDR block of 192.0.128.0/21 . What this means is that the first 21 bits of the 32 bits that form the IP address are part of the network. The remaining bits (11) are for the IP addresses in the VPC. Hit 'yes, Create' and it should create the VPC for you. When it creates the VPC it also creates a default route table and a default network ACL.

The default Route table allows access to instances within the VPC. It does not allow access to instances outside the VPC.

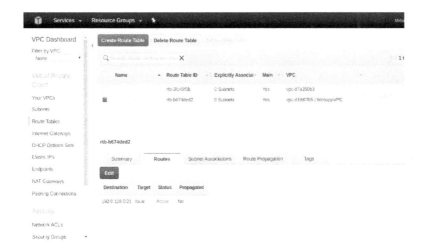

What is network ACL

VPC has two layers of security: security groups and network ACLs. Security Group can be allowed to modify permission any instance that it is attached to. ACLs, on the other hand, are applicable for the whole subnet that they are attached to. Also, ACL's are stateless so the rules for inbound and outbound traffic are separate. Amazon recommends using security groups as the first choice. The screenshot below shows the default ACL that allows all inbound traffic within the subnet.

Creating an AWS VPC Subnet Group

As shown in our network diagram, we will create four subnets spanning two Availability Zones(AZ). Each AZ will have one private and one public subnet. The idea is that if one AZ goes down, our system still works. Let's say, you are creating a web server, an application server and an RDS instance. We will have the RDS instance and the application server in the private subnet and the web server in the public subnet. This setup will be replicated in both AZ. We use a CIDR block of 129.0.12.0/24 for the first subnet. This would give us 251 usable IPs. Amazon reserves 5 addresses.

We similarly create the other three subnets.

Creating an AWS Internet Gateway

Two out of four of our Subnets are public. We need a gateway that allows the instances and services from the public subnet to access the internet. Here's how we create the gateway: click on the link on the left that says 'Internet Gateways'

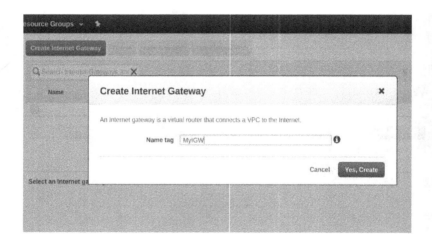

We call it 'MyIGW'.

Attaching an internet gateway to a VPC

When you create a new gateway it is in a detached state.

An Intenet Gateway needs to be attached to a VPC. We attach it to our VPC

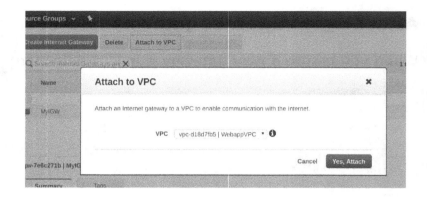

Adding route to a VPC

We will now create a new route table that allows instances inside a subnet to direct all traffic to the Internet gateway so that the gateway can direct it out to the internet. Click on 'Route Table' link on the left and then click on 'Create Route Table'

Add a new route that redirects all traffic (0.0.0.0/0) to the internet gateway that we created

As the last step we assign this route table to the subnets that we want to be public

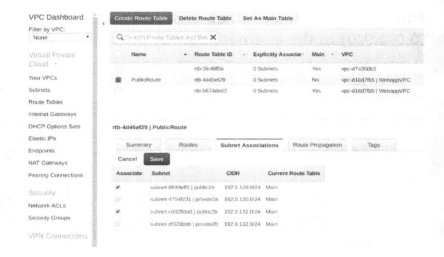

This finishes the second part of the tutorial. In the third and the last part we will look at how to create an Elastic IP address and assign that address to a NAT gateway so that instances in the private subnet can talk to the internet.

AWS VPC Elastic IP and NAT

In this AWS VPC Tutorial, we will learn how to create an Elastic IP address, a NAT Gateway, and accessing the internet from private subnet using the NAT gateway.

This is the third in the 3-series tutorial, the first tutorial introduced the key concepts and tutorial problem and the second tutorial looked at creating VPC, subnets, and internet gateway.

Why a NAT Gateway?

Before we explain why we need a NAT Gateway, here's a network diagram of what we are trying to accomplish.

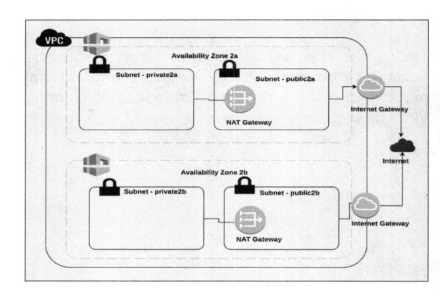

The two private networks need to talk to the internet for things like updating the operating system or installing software. Since the instances in the private network do not have a public IP, they need a NAT (Network Address Translation) Gateway that can convert the private IP to public IP for routing traffic to the internet and back. AWS provides two kinds of NAT resources – NAT instances and NAT gateways. The gateways are completely managed by AWS and so they are preferred over NAT instances.

What are Elastic IP Addresses

We will build a NAT gateway, however, the gateway needs an IP address. AWS provides Elastic IP addresses, that you can create on demand. These IP addresses can be attached to instances and resources and detached when not required.

Steps to create AWS Elastic IP Address

Click on Elastic IPs in the VPC console of AWS.

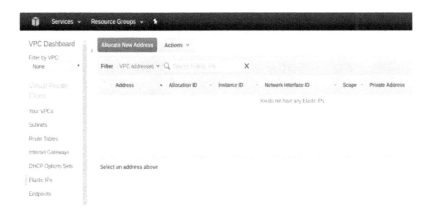

If you haven't created an IP address before you should see an empty table. Click on 'Allocate New Address' to add a new IP address. AWS will start creating the IP address for you.

Create two Elastic IPs for the two Gateways in each AZ.

	NAT Gateway	Status	Elastic IP Address	Private IP Address	Network Interface ID	VPC	Subnet	Created
	nat-32da9a...	Available	13.54.75.83	192.0.129.196	eni-9753bbdd	vpc-d18d7fb5	subnet-8649eff0	Novembe
■	nat-007df9d...	Available	13.54.88.226	192.0.129.56	eni-0259b148	vpc-d18d7fb5	subnet-8649eff0	Novembe

Steps to create the NAT gateway

Once the IP address is created, click on NAT Gateway to open up the NAT gateway homepage. Click on 'Create NAT Gateway' to create a new NAT Gateway. In The field that says 'Elastic IP Allocation ID' select the new IP that you just created and then hit 'Create NAT Gateway'. This will create the NAT Gateway.

Create a Route Table for NAT

The next step is to create the route table that will direct all traffic in the private subnet through the NAT Gateway. Click on the 'Route Table' section and click on 'Create Route Table'. In the Routes section, add a route that maps all traffic (0.0.0.0/0) to the NAT gateway that we just created.

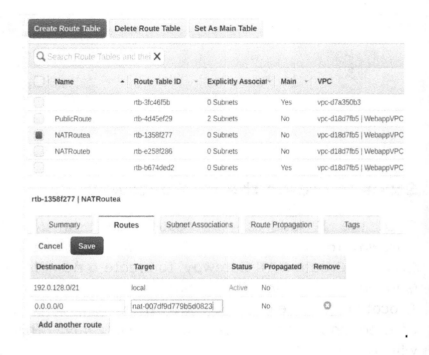

The Route table would need to be created for both the NAT Gateways.

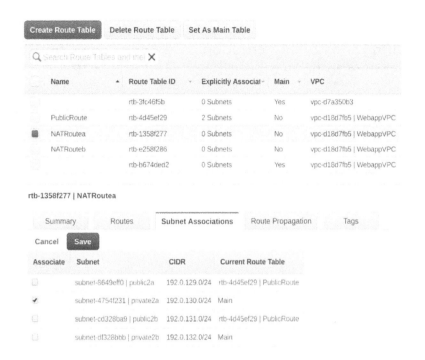

Recap of the AWS VPC Tutorial

Our first VPC setup is done. To recap, we created a VPC with four subnets. Two of the subnets were made public by attaching an internet gateway to it and the other two subnets were private. However, the private subnets were allowed to connect to the internet using a NAT gateway. The instances in the public subnet will have public IP addresses. We can configure the subnet to assign a public IP address to all instances that are created in the subnet, OR, during instance creation we can specify the instance to have an auto-assigned public IP.

Amazon S3 Bucket – Creation, Lifecycle, Version, Access

What is Amazon S3 bucket

Amazon S3 bucket (Simple Storage Service) is a storage service from Amazon where you can store and retrieve objects in the cloud using a web service. The web service operation can trigger functions such as lambda. A typical use case is where you store an image in the S3 bucket and as soon as you put the image in the bucket, it triggers a lambda that takes that image, generates a thumbnail and puts the thumbnail in another bucket. The object can be anything starting from a text file to a complete video file. The object can be as small as 1 byte or as large as 5 TB. You can store as many objects as you like.

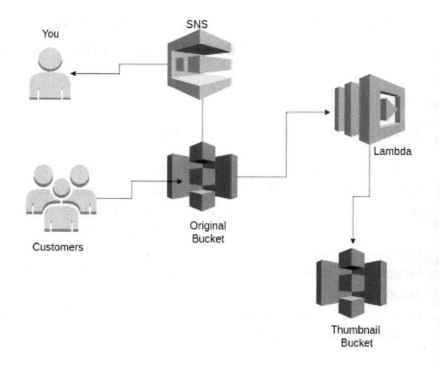

You

SNS

Lambda

Customers

Original
Bucket

Thumbnail
Bucket

Charges on Amazon S3 bucket

Amazon charges you for the actual storage, as well as for adding, retrieving or deleting objects.Each operation on the object is a web service call and each web service call is charged depending on the action that it performs.

What is a bucket

Buckets can be thought of as folders in a file system. Each bucket holds multiple objects. You can assign triggers to all operations in a bucket, so if you consider the earlier operation of generating a thumbnail then the original image can be in a bucket and the thumbnail can be in another bucket. If you put the thumbnail in the same bucket then it might again trigger a lambda which would create another thumbnail and so on and that would be an infinite loop. The name of each bucket is unique, so you cannot use a name that has been used by your account or any other account.

Permissions on S3 bucket

An S3 bucket or individual objects in the S3 bucket can be assigned permissions. Each user is called a 'Grantee' and the grantee can be assigned the following permissions for a bucket :

- List (List objects in the bucket)
- upload/delete (upload and delete object in the bucket
- View permissions
- Edit Permissions.

The grantee can be assigned the following permissions for an object

- Open/Download object
- View permissions on the object
- Edit the permissions of the object

Hosting a website using AWS S3 bucket

You can host an entire static website using Amazon S3 bucket. Each object in the bucket can be an HTML file or resources such as CSS,js, images etc. The resources can be accessed using the S3 bucket endpoint. However, in a real world, you would probably use Amazon CloudFront and combined with router 53 to redirect your domain to this end point.

Triggering Events from Amazon S3 bucket

This is probably the most powerful functionality. You can trigger events during events such as adding an object, deleting an object etc. These events could be an SNS topic, SQS queue or a Lambda function. A good use case is when your users upload a video file. You can store the video file as an object in a bucket. This would trigger a lambda function that would convert the video to various formats that can be used in multiple devices. You would also probably add a message in an SNS topic so that you get a mail whenever a new video is added or an SQS service so that you can the next available billing processor can process a bill for it.

Versioning of object in Amazon S3 bucket

The objects in the S3 buckets can be assigned a version. When you add another object with the same name, it is stored as the new version of the object. Each version is considered one object for billing purposes so you might want to consider deleting old versions. Once you enable versioning, you cannot disable it but only suspend it.

lifecycle of an object in Amazon S3 bucket

You can specify a lifecycle for all objects in a bucket of specific objects in a bucket (identified by a prefix). The lifecycle allows you to add rules to delete the object after a specified time. It also allows you to move the object to different kinds of storage such as infrequently accessed storage and then delete it, if required. If you enable versioning, then the main object and the versioned objects can have different lifecycles.

Cross Region Replication of S3 object

You can enable cross region replication of all objects in S3 bucket. What this means is that Amazon would store a copy of your object in a different region. This makes your object highly available even if one region goes down. Imagine that you are a weather company and you store weather images in the bucket. If there is a storm the data center of a region might go down, but since you have a backup in another region, you can start using that.

Tags, requester pays and Transfer acceleration

Tags allow you to add key value pairs to the bucket and this allows you generate billing reports grouped by tags. For example. you can tag one bucket as "Project A" and then you can work out the total cost of S3 buckets for Project A in your bills.

If you allow a different account to perform operations on your bucket then you can enable Requester Pays to let that account pay for the usage and data transfer charges on the bucket.

As claimed by Amazon, transfer Acceleration makes data transfer in and out of the bucket faster and there is an extra charge for it.

Create AWS EC2 instance using CLI

In the previous tutorial we saw how to create AWS EC2 instance using the console. In this tutorial, we will learn how to create AWS EC2 instance using the CLI (Command Line Interface).

create AWS EC2 instance using CLI

What is Amazon CLI

Amazon CLI stands for Amazon Client Line Interface. It is a command line tool to perform most of the functions that you can perform on the Amazon Console. The advantage of the tool is that it allows you to write scripts to perform most of the tasks and also gives a chance to automate repeated tasks. Before we start using the amazon CLI we need to get the access Key ID and the secret key.

Steps to get the Amazon AWS access key ID and secret key

1. Go to the IAM Console and click on Users.

2. Click on the User that you want to create the access key for. Click on the actual row and not the check box.
3. On the next screen, click on "Create Access Key". If you have created keys before you should be able to see them (but can't download them again)
4. You will see a popup that allows you to download the access ID and key. The keys can be downloaded only once so make sure you save it in a safe place. You can, however, create another key later on.
5. The downloaded CSV has both the access id and key.

Install Amazon CLI (Command Line Interface) on unix

Now that you have the access ID and key, the next step is to install the Amazon CLI (Command Line Interface). In this tutorial, we will show you how to install it on a unix machine.

The installation is quite straightforward. Follow these three steps to install it:

```
curl "https://s3.amazonaws.com/aws-cli/awscli-bundle.zip" -o "awscli-bundle.zip"
unzip awscli-bundle.zip
```

```
./awscli-bundle/install -b ~/bin/aws
```

Configure Amazon CLI (Command Line Interface)

Once you install the CLI, the next step is to configure it. Configuration involves setting up the access ID and key and the default region so that you can then start using the CLI for creating the EC2 instance (amongst other things)

Here are the steps

1. Type in "aws configure" on the command line.
2. Enter the Access ID, key and the default region.
3. That configures the CLI. This creates a directory called .aws in home. This directory has the credentials and the config file.
4. To test the configuration we will create a security group and then delete it from the AWS console. To create the security group type in.

"aws ec2 create-security-group --group-name my-sg --description "My security group"

5. This will create a new security group. Logon to AWS console to double check if you can see the security group (under EC2). You can then delete the group.

Create AWS EC2 instance using CLI

We now finally look at how to create the EC2 instance using CLI. The CLI command for creating instance is called run-instances. When you create an instance from the console, you go through seven steps of configuration. All of that can be done using specific parameters on the CLI. While creating the instance we want to be able to select the AMI (machine image); select the instance type (hardware); set the VPC, IAM role, and other configuration parameters; configure additional block storage; add tags; add security groups and then launch one or multiple instances. Let's see what parameters we need to set to configure each of the above:

Option	Example	description
--dry-run	--dry-run true	Check permission without making actual request.
--image-id	--image-id ami-5ec1673e	The Amazon Image to use to create the instance.
--key-name	--key-name MyKey	The Key pair to use to SSH to the server.
--security-groups	--security-groups EC2SecurityGroup	The security group for the EC2 instance. Default group is used if none specified
--instance-type	--instance-type t2.micro	The hardware for the instance.

--placement	--placement AvailabilityZone: us-east-1b	place the server in us-east-1b zone
--block-device-mappings	--block-device-mappings DeviceName=/dev/sdh,Ebs={VolumeSize=100}	Use an additional block storage of 100G and mount it at /dev/sdh. This is in addition to root volume.
--count	--count 2	Launch two instances.

The table above specifies only some of the options. Look at this link to look at all the options. (http://docs.aws.amazon.com/cli/latest/reference/ec2/run-instances.html)

Create an AWS security group using command line.

Before we create the EC2 instance, lets create the security group from the command line.

The first command creates the security group. Once that is done the next command adds a rule that opens up port 22 for SSH for all users. In real world scenario you would use a fixed IP or fixed range of IPs. The last command shows the security group created.

```
aws ec2 create-security-group --group-name
EC2SecurityGroup --description "Security Group for EC2
instances to allow port 22"

aws ec2 authorize-security-group-ingress --group-name
EC2SecurityGroup --protocol tcp --port 22 --cidr
0.0.0.0/0

aws ec2 describe-security-groups --group-names
EC2SecurityGroup
```

Command to Create AWS EC2 instance using CLI

Finally, here is the command to create the EC2 instance using the CLI.

```
aws ec2 run-instances   --image-id ami-5ec1673e --key-name
MyKey --security-groups EC2SecurityGroup --instance-type
t2.micro --placement AvailabilityZone=us-west-2b --block-
device-mappings
DeviceName=/dev/sdh,Ebs={VolumeSize=100} --count 2
```

This creates two instances and here's how the two instances look.

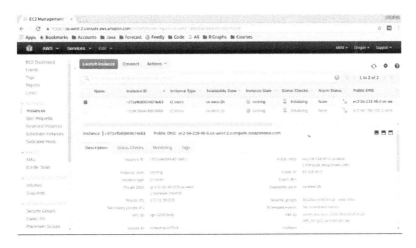

This completes our tutorial on creating the EC2 instances using the CLI. The run-instances method has many options that cover most of the situations. Look at <u>this</u> amazon doc link for reference.

Amazon Elastic Cloud Compute (EC2) – Creating an Instance

This tutorial walks through the steps of creating an Amazon Elastic Cloud Compute (EC2) instance. We will create a unix instance that is available in the free tier.

Steps to create an Amazon Elastic Cloud Compute (EC2) instance.

Step 0 : EC2 Launch Instance page

The first step is to go to the EC2 dashboard. Once you login to Amazon EC2 you should be able to see a link called EC2 in the welcome page or the Services page. Click on that link and you should see this page :

This page gives an overview of the current instances in your account, current storage volumes used and some other services that we will see later on. For now, let's just go ahead and create an instance. Click on "Launch Instance" to create your first instance. The next step is to create the type of machine that you want to create.

Step 1 : Amazon EC2 select the Amazon Machine Image (AMI)

You can create Amazon EC2 instances with various type of operating systems. Step 1 asks you to select the operating system that you want the EC2 instance to have. There is a checkbox on the left that allows you to select the instances available in the free tier. On this page, you would have noticed that the first kind of operating system is Amazon Linux AMI. This provides amazon managed UNIX that is updated regularly; has repository access to certain softwares such as mysql, apache etc.; has included packages that ease integration with other amazon instances such as the Amazon CLI. Let's use this for our tutorial

There are other tabs on this page that allow you to create instances from images in the Amazon marketplace. we will look at them in a later tutorial.

Step 2 : Amazon EC2 – Choose an instance type

In this step we select the hardware configuration that we want for the server. There are five different classes of hardware configuration – General Purpose, Compute Optimized, GPU Compute, Memory Optimized and Storage Optimized. They all serve different purposes. For example, you would use a compute optimized server if you have a web application that receives a high amount of traffic. Within each class, you can select a server depending on the number of cores it has and the memory (RAM). Some classes of servers such as General purpose do not have any storage space and you have to add them later on. This storage space is called Elastic Block Storage. Let's select the 'free tier eligible' type for this tutorial. It has 1 cpu and 1G of memory.

Step 3 : Amazon EC2 – Configure Instance details

The first option allows you to create more than one instance or make it a part of auto scaling group so that amazon can add or remove similar instances based on the work load. We will look at this later, for now we need one instance and no auto scaling group.

Amazon AWS has a payment option where you can bid for spot instances. This is hardware that amazon allows you to use when their hardware is underutilized. It could be much cheaper than the normal rates. However, you have no control over when amazon would create that instance and when it would delete it. We don't use it for this tutorial.

We can select the VPC and the network that it belongs to. Chose the defaults now and in a later tutorial we will look at VPCs.

You could add a role to the AWS instance so that it comes with a pre-defined set of permissions. Note that the role cannot be added later on so if you need one, add it now. For this tutorial, we don't add anything.

You can specify whether the instance should be stopped on shutdown or terminated. We will select terminated.

The next step is to add storage to the server

Step 4 : Amazon EC2 – Add Block Storage

With the General Purpose servers you can add as
much block storage as you require. Block storage is
just like a hard disk. There are three flavors of
block storages – General Purpose SSD, Provisioned
IOPS SSD and magnetic. For our use General
purpose will suffice.

Step 5 : Amazon EC2 – Tag Instance

You can apply custom tags to instances. These tags
are useful when you want to generate usage or
billing reports based on certain criteria. For

example, we can tag the instances with departments and then its easy to generate usage or billing report for a particular department.

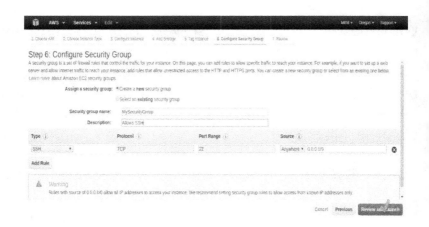

Step 6 : Amazon EC2 – Configure Security Group

Amazon provides security groups that are like firewall rules. Security groups are an easy way to provide access to various ports of the machine. In our example we just want to allow access to port 22 for SSH. we can allow access from all machines or from a particular IP. The interface provides a dropdown in the first column that provides an easy way to select access rules for various protocols. Once we creat a security group, we can reuse it for other servers. In our example, we haven't created any security group yet, so select the check box that says 'Create a new security group'. If you have already created a group previously then reuse that if it has ssh enabled. We call it 'MyEC2SecurityGroup'. Click on 'Review and Launch

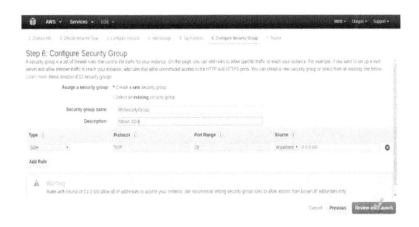

Step 7 : Amazon EC2 – Review Instance launch

This step allows you to review your configurations. You will see a message if your security group allows ssh from all machines. For production machines, we generally allow access from a particular IP only. For this tutorial, its ok to ignore that message. click on 'launch' to launch your first instance

Step 8 : Amazon EC2 – Key pair

Amazon uses a key pair file to login to the server. When you hit launch, you will be presented with a popup that asks you to use an existing key pair or create a new one. If you have already created a server, you can use the key pair that you created for that server or you can opt to create a new one.

We put in the name "MyKey" and click on *Download Key Pair*. Save the file somewhere on your machine. Note the path where you stored the

key pair. Click on "Launch Instances" once you have downloaded the file. You Should see a message that says that your instances are being created.

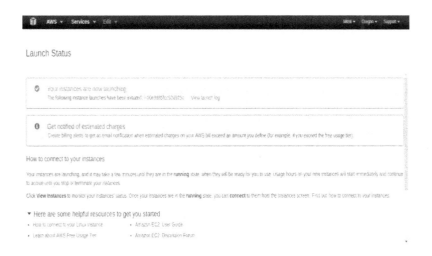

If you go back to the EC2 dashboard you should see that the number of EC2 instances has increased.

Step 9 : Amazon EC2 – Login to the server

Now that we have created the server lets see how to login to the server. Open up a terminal window and go to the folder where you have downloaded the key pair. If you use windows, you might have to use putty to ssh. This tutorial assumes Unix. The first thing to do is to change the permission level for the key pair file. We do that using this command

To login to the server use this command :

```
chmod 400 MyKey.pem
```

To login to the server use this command :

```
ssh -i "MyKey.pem" ec2-user@&lt;yourserver&gt;
```

```
  ec2-user@ip-172-31-6-170:~
ithil@mithil:~/studytrails/amazon$ ls
C2  MyKey.pem  st_fz  studytrails.pem
ithil@mithil:~/studytrails/amazon$ chmod 400 MyKey.pem
ithil@mithil:~/studytrails/amazon$ ssh -i "MyKey.pem" ec2-user@ec2-54-214-121-1
1.us-west-2.compute.amazonaws.com
he authenticity of host 'ec2-54-214-121-121.us-west-2.compute.amazonaws.com (54
214.121.121)' can't be established.
CDSA key fingerprint is 58:ac:9b:2e:69:92:66:58:10:98:e3:d3:55:e4:ae:3a.
re you sure you want to continue connecting (yes/no)? yes
arning: Permanently added 'ec2-54-214-121-121.us-west-2.compute.amazonaws.com,5
.214.121.121' (ECDSA) to the list of known hosts.

    _|  _|_  )
    _| (    /    Amazon Linux AMI
    _|\___|___|

ttps://aws.amazon.com/amazon-linux-ami/2016.09-release-notes/
 package(s) needed for security, out of 10 available
un "sudo yum update" to apply all updates.
```

To shutdown the server from the terminal type in

```
sudo shutdown now
```

Terminate the instance from the console. Note that when you delete the instance the EBS volume that is used as the root volume is also deleted, however any other volume that you add will not be deleted.

That finishes this tutorial on creating the first EC2 instance. In the next tutorial we look at how to use the Amazon CLI to create instances.

Amazon Elastic Cloud Compute (EC2) – Introduction

This tutorial gives an introduction to Amazon EC2 Instance.

What is Amazon Elastic Cloud Compute (EC2)

Amazon Elastic Cloud Compute (EC2) is a service from Amazon that allows you to create machines in the cloud on-demand. Traditionally, the procedure for obtaining a new machine is probably not an alien concept to anyone reading this tutorial. You need to figure out what configuration is required and then fill out the paperwork and then wait patiently for your machine to arrive. All good, but now you realize that you probably don't need that machine for one month. Can you return it and then reorder it after a month? probably not. Amazon (and the other cloud providers) allows you to create servers on the cloud such that you only pay for the number of hours of usage.

So let's say that you wake up on Monday morning and you realize that it's a wonderful day and you are in the mood of creating something new. Maybe you want to quickly whip up an environment and see how that site that you have been working on for months performs on a real server. Amazon has got you covered. Go to your console and click a few buttons and in 5 minutes you have a server. ssh into it, install the web server, copy your website code and see how it looks. Now if you want to kill the server so that you can go back to coding, then just hit another button and the server is gone for good. Of course, you can create an image if required so that the next time you don't have to install all of those servers again. Amazon just charges you for the closest hour that you use the server for.

Features of Amazon Cloud Computer (EC2)

Here are some of the features of Amazon Cloud Compute (EC2)

- You can create servers with windows and various formats of Unix.
- You can create servers from AWS marketplace that has around 1800 different kinds server images that you can use to create your own server. For example, there is

an instance called "WordPress powered by Bitnami" that allows you to create an image that has WordPress installed and ready to use.

- The servers are charged by the hour so if you use it for 2.5 hours you get billed for 3 hours.
- You can select from a long list of server configurations. The configurations allow use to chose a server based on the usage. There are general purpose servers, compute optimized, GPU-optimized, memory optimized and Storage optimized servers.
- You can attach more storage to the server, even after the server has been created and used for some time. You can similarly remove storage from it.
- You can have firewall kind of access control over it using security groups

These are some of the key features of EC2 instances. There are many more and we will see some of them in the next tutorials. For now, the next tutorial shows you how to create your first instance.

Mount Amazon Elastic File System (EFS) to EC2

This chapter shows how to Mount Amazon Elastic File System (EFS) to EC2 on Amazon AWS. For those of you who don't know what EFS and EC2 are, here's a one line introduction.

One line introduction to Amazon Elastic File System (EFS) and Amazon EC2

EFS – Elastic File System

– Amazon EFS is a file system then can store petabytes of data and that can be mounted to multiple amazon EC2 machines. The File system is independent of the server.

AMazon EC2

– Amazon EC2 instances are amazon virtual private machines that you can use as a computer on the cloud.

Steps to mount EFS on EC2

Creating an Elastic File System

Login to Amazon AWS management console and click on EFS. If this is the first time you are using EFS then you should see the welcome screen

Hit on create file system. The next page showw "configure file system access". chose the default and click "Next Stemp"

Hit Next and Step 2 says Configure optional settings. You can add key-value tags on this page. The tags can be used later for reports or billing breakdown.

The last step is to review and create the File
System.

Once you hit create the file system will be created.
It will also create mount targets for

Creating The Security Groups For Elastic File System (EFS) and EC2

The next step after creating the EFS is creating the security groups for EFS and EC2. We want to be able to mount an EFS on EC2, which means we are looking at opening up two kinds of firewalls (look at security groups as opening up of firewall ports)

- Opening up the port on EFS so that EC2 can connect to it.
- Opening up the SSH port on EC2 so that we can connect to it.

Lets first look at how to create the security group to allow connection to EFS. Open up the EC2 dashboard and look at security groups section on the left menu.

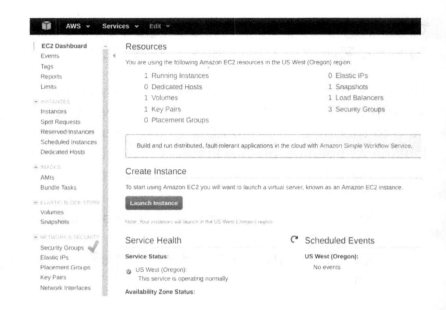

On the security groups page click on 'Create Security Group'

You shoud see a create Security group popup. Enter a security group name. We have used 'EFSSecurityGroup'; Add a description; we choose the default VPC; Add an InBound rule with type as NFS, it should auto populate protocol and port range; We select a source of 'Anywhere' from the dropdown but you can limit it to a particular IP; click on create.

Create another security group for the EC2 instances. We use 'EC2SecurityGroup' for the name; Add an new inbound rule for SSH and source 'Anywhere' or a specific IP if you so choose.

Assigning appropriate groups to the Elastic File System (EFS) and EC2

We have created the groups and now the next step is to add the groups to EFS and EC2. Go to the EFS group and click on 'Mange File System Access'. Remove the default Security Groups and add the 'EFSSecurityGroup' and click on save.

Similarly, assign the 'EC2SecurityGroup' to the EC2 instance.

Mounting the Elastic File System (EFS) to EC2

The last step now is to mount the file system to EC2. If you go to the file system dashboard, you should see a link that has instructions to mount the file system. Click on the link to bring up up this window

EC2 mount instructions

> sudo yum install -y nfs-utils
> - On an Ubuntu instance
> sudo apt-get install nfs-common

Mounting your file system

1. Open an SSH client and connect to your EC2 instance. (find out how to connect)
2. Create a new directory on your EC2 instance, such as "efs".
   - sudo mkdir efs
3. Mount your file system using the DNS name. The following command looks up your EC2 instance's Availability Zone (AZ) using the EC2 instance metadata URI 169.254.169.254, then mounts the file system using the DNS name for that AZ. What is EC2 instance metadata? | Mounting considerations)
   - sudo mount -t nfs4 -o nfsvers=4.1,rsize=1048576,wsize=1048576,hard,timeo=600,retrans=2 $(curl -s http://169.254.169.254/latest/meta-data/placement/availability-zone).fs-55ba41fc.efs.us-west-2.amazonaws.com:/ efs

If you are unable to connect, please see our troubleshooting documentation.

If you have created the EC2 instance using the Amazon linux then you should have the required tools to mount the file system. If not, follow the instructions on the popup; create a folder called 'efs' on the EC2 instance and fire the command specified on step 3 of the popup to mount it. If you copy paste the command directly it should work fine. To permanently mount the EFS add the entry to /etc/fstab file

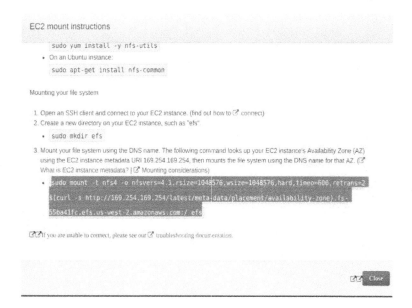

Once you mount the file system, you can start creating files to it. Also, If you unmount the file system and mount it to a different machine the files are all still there. To unmount the file system type in 'sudo umount efs/'

```
[ec2-user@ip-172-31-28-181 ~]$ ls
efs
[ec2-user@ip-172-31-28-181 ~]$ sudo mount -t nfs4 -o nfsvers=4.1,rsize=1048576,w
size=1048576,hard,timeo=600,retrans=2 $(curl -s http://169.254.169.254/latest/me
ta-data/placement/availability-zone).fs-55ba41fc.efs.us-west-2.amazonaws.com:/ e
fs
[ec2-user@ip-172-31-28-181 ~]$ cd efs
[ec2-user@ip-172-31-28-181 efs]$ touch a.txt
touch: cannot touch 'a.txt': Permission denied
[ec2-user@ip-172-31-28-181 efs]$ sudo touch a.txt
[ec2-user@ip-172-31-28-181 efs]$ ls
a.txt
[ec2-user@ip-172-31-28-181 efs]$ sudo umount efs/
umount: efs/: mountpoint not found
[ec2-user@ip-172-31-28-181 efs]$ cd ..
[ec2-user@ip-172-31-28-181 ~]$ sudo umount efs/
[ec2-user@ip-172-31-28-181 ~]$ cd efs
[ec2-user@ip-172-31-28-181 efs]$ ls
[ec2-user@ip-172-31-28-181 efs]$ cd ..
[ec2-user@ip-172-31-28-181 ~]$ sudo mount -t nfs4 -o nfsvers=4.1,rsize=1048576,w
size=1048576,hard,timeo=600,retrans=2 $(curl -s http://169.254.169.254/latest/me
ta-data/placement/availability-zone).fs-55ba41fc.efs.us-west-2.amazonaws.com:/ e
fs
[ec2-user@ip-172-31-28-181 ~]$ cd efs
[ec2-user@ip-172-31-28-181 efs]$ ls
a.txt
[ec2-user@ip-172-31-28-181 efs]$
```

That finishes the tutorial on mounting the EFS to EC2.

How To Launch An AWS EC2 Server and Set Up Ubuntu 16.04 On It

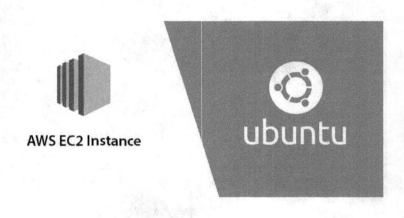

AWS EC2 Instance

In this tutorial, We will learn how to setup an AWS EC2 Instance from scratch. We will configure the Ubuntu 16.04 OS on the server. Also we will do some essential configuration like setting up the hostname, correct locale and NTP service.

This requires the following steps:

For this particular tutorial, I have logged into my AWS EC2 account in N.Virginia zone.

When you Go to > EC2 dashboard. Here, In case we have no instances running (0 Running Instances), we need Go to > instances and select **Launch Instances**.

Step no.1 - Choose an Amazon Machine Image (Ami)

Go to > **Ubuntu Server 16.04 Lts (HVM), SSD, Volume type-ami- 2ef48339**, which is the latest Ami from Ubuntu and which will have support for next 5 years (approx).
Select and use > 64-bit version.

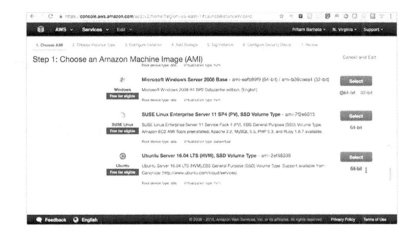

Step no.2 - Choose an Instance Type

For this tutorial,
Use a t2.micro instance (low to moderate). Go to>
Next

Step no.3 - Configure Instance Details

Here number of instance is '1'. Let it be as default VPC and the default Subnet.

Go to > 'Shutdown Behavior'.

For Production server,in option 'Shutdown Behavior', let it be as 'stop'.

Go to > 'Protect Against Accidental Termination' and enable it, in order to prevent server being terminated quite easily.

Here, We are not going to enable 'CloudWatch Detailed Monitoring'.

Go to> Add storage

Step no.4 - Add Storage

By default, EC2 comes with an 8 GiB disk size

8GiB is not sufficient for most of the server scenarios as you want to have some room for things like log files and backups. So we need to choose a provision for 25 GiB disk space in general.

Always use **General Purpose SSD (GP2)** unless you have a reason to choose a '**Magnetic**' Disk.

'**Provisional IOPS SSD (IO1)** is a specialized type of disk which is very expensive and should be used only for high performance database requirements with the client approval.

You should use 'Delete On Termination' always.

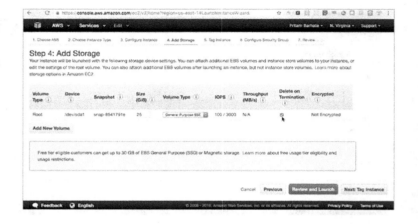

This way it will be ensured that this volume would be deleted once the server is deleted.

Step no. 5 - Tag Instance

Give a good name to the server. Good policy is to use the final domain name that you're going to assign to the server.

```
# Basic Server Setup

# Set the hostname
echo "demosetup" | sudo tee /etc/hostname
sudo hostname -F /etc/hostname

# Set the Fully Qualified Domain Name (FQDN)

vi /etc/hosts

127.0.0.1 localhost.localdomain localhost
[ip] demosetup.mobisoftinfotech.com demosetup
```

Step no. 6 - Configure Security Group

By default, generally you have one Security Group but you should create a new Security Group as per the purpose of the server. For example, you might want to create Security Group for Web servers differently from that of the database servers.

I am going to create a new Security Group and name it as **"WebServers"** and change the description to **"WebServers Security Group"**

By default, this allows you to have SSH access. From here, you can control the sources, as in, from where the users would be able to do SSH login. So, for general servers, we keep it to "Anywhere"

Step no. 7 - Review and Launch

Review and if everything is in order, then select 'Launch'. When you select 'Launch' a pop up will appear which will give you an option of either using existing Key Pair or create a new Key Pair.

It is generally preferred that instead of using the same key pair for all servers, you should create a new one for certain groups of servers. Though, you might want to keep one key pair per account where you need to have only 3-4 servers per account which might be the case for small webapps.

Now, for creating a new Key pair
Go to > " Create a new pair" and then name it as
'demoserver'.

Download the newly created Key Pair. Once, it is
downloaded, you can *Launch* Instance.

Once the server get launched we can login using
SSH. For that, I would require to access the Pem
file. If you run this command, you might see that
the permission for the Pem file is-
rw-r--r—

This means that other people can also read this
Pem file. This is not allowed for SSH Pem files. So,
we will have to change the permission for this Pem
file to 400.

```
$ chmod 400 demoserver.pem
```

Now, only the current user can read this Pem file and these are permission that a Pem file expects.

```
Last login: Sun Oct  9 15:49:42 on ttys000
Pritams-MacBook-Pro:~ pritam$ cd /Users/pritam/Downloads/Chrome
Pritams-MacBook-Pro:Chrome pritam$ ls
demoserver.pem
Pritams-MacBook-Pro:Chrome pritam$ ls -la
total 24
drwxr-xr-x   4 pritam  staff   136 Oct  9 16:26 .
drwx------  11 pritam  staff   374 Oct  7 19:41 ..
-rw-r--r--@  1 pritam  staff  6148 Oct  9 16:26 .DS_Store
-rw-r--r--@  1 pritam  staff  1696 Oct  9 16:24 demoserver.pem
Pritams-MacBook-Pro:Chrome pritam$ chmod 400 demoserver.pem
Pritams-MacBook-Pro:Chrome pritam$ ls -la
total 24
drwxr-xr-x   4 pritam  staff   136 Oct  9 16:26 .
drwx------  11 pritam  staff   374 Oct  7 19:41 ..
-rw-r--r--@  1 pritam  staff  6148 Oct  9 16:26 .DS_Store
-r--------@  1 pritam  staff  1696 Oct  9 16:24 demoserver.pem
Pritams-MacBook-Pro:Chrome pritam$ 
```

Now, our server is running but it doesn't have the Elastic IPs.

In ec2, when you stop a server and start it all over again, the Public IP of the server changes. This is generally not desirable for most of the deployment. So, in this case, you would want to assign an Elastic IP address which doesn't change during server stop/start.

For this, Go to> Elastic IPs and select 'Allocate a new address'.

Right click on the newly allocated address and choose 'Associate Address'. In this, select the name of the server you want to associate the IP address with. In this case I will choose i-02719532.

Now, I'll login to server:

```
$ ssh -i demoserver.pem ubuntu@50.17.127.41
```

Since, I am in the same directory where the Pem file is present. I do not need the full path for the pem file.
I would now require to setup a hostname with this command

```
$ echo $HOST_NAME | sudo tee /etc/hostname
```
This basically, inserts "demosetup" word in '/etc/hostname' path.

After this, run

```
$ sudo hostname -F /etc/hostname
```

So, if we restart the server we will see this hostname reflected here (instead of the IP) but before that we will run some more commands. So that we do not have to restart time and again.

The setting up of Fully Qualified Domain Name (FQDN) is optional but is a good to have practise so that if some server software depends on this FQDN then it will find it here.

Though, it is good to have the FQDN setup to the final sub-domain that you would want to the server to have, it is not really required. It can be any arbitrary FQDN. So, I'll first have to edit following file:

    $ sudo vi /etc/hosts

Then we need to add the following line below the localhost line that should be already present in the file:

50.17.127.41   demosetup.mobisoftinfotech.com demosetup

Next, Upgrade the system
Run the command:

    $ sudo apt-get update

'apt-get update command' updates sources for various packages. The actual upgrade happens with the upgrade command. To upgrade the installed packages run:

    $ sudo apt-get upgrade

It is a good practise to update your system before doing any other setup so that all the security patches are applied to the server.

Now, we should **Set the locale** for the system. And we will set the locale to **en_US.UTF-8**'

This is very important for database systems so that if you're supporting multilingual databases, the data is represented correctly.

```
$ echo 'LC_ALL=en_US.UTF-8' | sudo tee -a
/etc/environment

$ echo 'LANG=en_US.UTF-8' | sudo tee -a
/etc/environment
```

This service ensures the clock is always synchronized with the remote servers. This will always give you perfect time for all data related operations.

This is important mainly for database system as well as for programs which need date calculations. Almost all enterprises systems need correct date to be setup on the server. So, this is very important to configure on the server.

Now we need to force the system clock to sync with the NTP. For that we need to run following commands:

```
$ sudo service ntp stop
$ sudo ntpdate -s time.nist.gov
$ sudo service ntp start
```

Now, we are ready to restart our system.
We will run the command to 'restart the system':

```
$ sudo init 6
```

We will have to wait for a couple of minutes for our system to reboot. Once the system is up and running, do the SSH login and you can see that the hostname is set to demosetup.

At this point, our **Basic server setup** is complete!

Virtual Private Cloud (VPC) Best Configuration Practices

Many ask questions about basic AWS security issues, including those addressed by using Virtual Private Clouds (VPCs). So in this chapter we provide a guide for setting up and using VPCs in order to help guide your AWS setup. This AWS VPC tutorial is based on our experience from using VPN in AWS deployments for internal systems and for customers' systems. VyScale, our cost- and performance-management solution, is an excellent tool for setting up systems inside of VPCs.

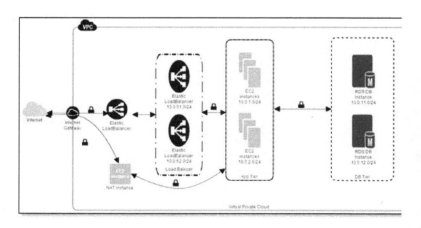

A VPC is a virtual network dedicated to your AWS account that's logically isolated from other virtual networks in the AWS cloud. You can launch your AWS resources, such as Amazon EC2, RDS, ElasticCache and other instances into your VPC.

For information about the number of VPCs you can create, see **Amazon VPC Limits**.

http://docs.aws.amazon.com/AmazonVPC/latest/UserGuide/VPC_Appendix_Limits.html_)

AWS VPC Setup

Create VPC

Log in to the AWS console.

Navigate to Services->VPC->Your VPCs.

Click "**Create VPC**".

When you create an Amazon AWS VPC, you specify a set of IP addresses in the form of a Classless Inter-Domain Routing (CIDR) block (for example, 10.0.0.0/16). For more information about CIDR notation and what "/16" means, see **Classless Inter-Domain Routing**.

You can assign a single CIDR block to a VPC. The allowed block size is between a /28 netmask and /16 netmask. In other words, the VPC can contain from 16 to 65,536 IP addresses.

You cannot change a VPC's size after creating it. If your VPC is too small for your needs, you'll need to terminate all of the instances in the VPC, delete it, and then create a new, larger VPC.

To create your VPC, go to the Create VPC dialog box, specify the following VPC details and then click "**Yes, Create**".

CIDR Block: Specify the CIDR block for your VPC. I prefer 10.0.0.0/16.

Tenancy: Default tenancy: This is for running instances on shared hardware and is is free of charge.

Dedicated Tenancy: This is for running your instances on single-tenant hardware. A $2 fee applies for each hour in which any dedicated instance is running in a region.

Create VPC   Cancel ×

A VPC is an isolated portion of the AWS cloud populated by AWS objects, such as Amazon EC2 instances. Please use the Classless Inter-Domain Routing (CIDR) block format to specify your VPC's contiguous IP address range, for example, 10.0.0.0/16. Please note that you can create a VPC no larger than /16.

CIDR Block: 10.0.0.0/16   (e.g. 10.0.0.0/16)

Tenancy: Default ⌄

                                   Cancel   Yes, Create

Creating Subnets

In the navigation pane click on "**Subnets**".

Click "**Create Subnet**".

Before we create a subnet, let's understand the best practices for creating them.

You should create subnets across multiple availability zones, with each subnet residing within a single zone. Creating subnets in and launching instances across multiple availability zones will ensure a high-availability environment.

When creating separate subnets for ELB, EC2 and RDS instances, each tier should have at least 2 subnets across availability zones.

For this example, we created subnets using zones us-east1b and us-east-1d. These subnets are called "private subnets" because the instances we launch are not accessible from the Internet. In other words, these instances don't have a public IP unless you assign an EIP.

App Tier: 10.0.1.0/24(zone-b), 10.0.2.0/24(zone-d)

ELB: 10.0.51.0/24(zone-b), 10.0.52.0/24(zone-d)

Database (RDS): 10.0.11.0/24(zone-b), 10.0.12.0/24(zone-d)

Always choose the same Amazon Availability Zones for all tiers. For example, if you choose two zones for high availability and use us-east-1a and us-east1b, then maintain those same 1a and 1b zones for all tiers. This will minimize data transfer charges because data transfers between instances within the same availability zone are free.

Create Subnet   Cancel ✕

Please use the CIDR format to specify your subnet's IP address block (e.g., 10.0.0.0/24). Please note that block sizes must be between a /16 netmask and /28 netmask. Also, please note that a subnet can be the same size as your VPC.

VPC: vpc-1a233c78 (10.0.0.0/16) ▾

Availability Zone: us-east-1a ▾

CIDR Block: 10.0.1.0/24   (e.g. 10.0.0.0/24)

[Cancel] [Yes, Create]

Create AWS Internet Gateway

By default, instances that are launched into a VPC can't communicate with the Internet. However, you can enable Internet access by attaching an Internet gateway to the VPC.

Go to Internet Gateways in the navigation pane and click "**Create Internet Gateway**".

Now attach the gateway to a VPC by right clicking on "VPC" and selecting "**Attach to VPC**".

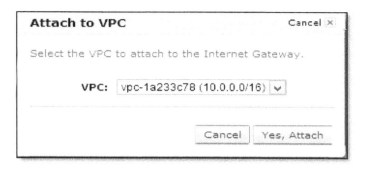

Create Route Tables

A route table contains a set of rules, called routes, that determine where network traffic is directed.

Each subnet in your VPC must be associated with a route table that will control that subnet's routing. You can associate multiple subnets with a single route table; however, you can only associate a subnet with one route table.

Creating a VPC automatically creates a main route table which, by default, enables the instances in your VPC to communicate with one other.

Go to Route Tables in the navigation pane and click on "**Create Route Table**".

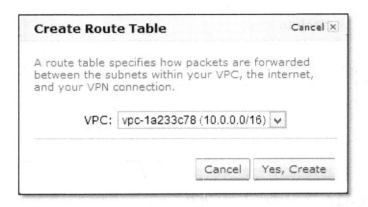

As a best practice create separate route tables for each tier. This will provide more control in maintaining the security of each subnet.

Now associate the subnets to the route tables. Click on one route table and go to the Associations tab. Select the subnet and click "**Associate**".

Associate each tier's subnets separately to the dedicated route table.

Create 3 new route tables:

1. **ELB Route table**—Associate 10.0.51.0/24 and 10.0.52.0/24.
2. **APP route table**—Associate 10.0.1.0/24 and 10.0.2.0/24.

3. **RDS route table**—Associate 10.0.11.0/24 and 10.0.12.0/24.

Do not associate any subnets with the main route table. Now navigate to the main route table to add a route to allow Internet traffic to the VPC. Go to Routes and specify the following values:

Destination: 0.0.0.0/0

Target: Select "Internet Gateway" from the dropdown menu.

Create AWS Security Groups

This process is similar to creating an SG (Security Group) in classic EC2.

Create separate security groups for ELB, APP, DB (RDS) and NAT instances.

1. APP_SG01
2. NAT_SG01
3. ELB_SG01
4. DB_SG01

Allow Inbound rules for ELB, DB and APP to suit your needs. We'll address NAT security group rules later in this book.

Create NAT instance

Instances launched into a private subnet in a VPC cannot communicate with the Internet unless you assign a public IP or EIP to the instance. However, assigning a public IP to an instance will allow everyone to initiate inbound Internet traffic.

Using a Network Address Translation (NAT) instance in your VPC enables instances in the private subnet to initiate outbound Internet traffic.

Create a subnet with netmask 10.0.0.0/24 for NAT instance]. We call this subnet a "public subnet" and the others "private subnets". While, technically, there is no difference between public or private subnet, for clarity we call publicly accessible instances public subnets.

Associate this subnet to the main route table. You can also create separate route tables to associate to the subnet. If you do create a separate route table, don't forget to add a route that will allow Internet traffic into the subnet.

Now navigate to Services->EC2->Launch Instance

In the Launch Wizard select "**Community AMIs**" and search for "**ami-vpc-nat**". " Select the first AMI from the results list to launch the instance into the VPC created in section #1. Choose the subnet 10.0.0.0/24 and then check the "Assign public IP" box. You can also assign an EIP, if needed. On the Configure Security Group page, choose "Select an existing security group" and select the NAT_SG security group that you created earlier.

Number of instances ⓘ	1	
Purchasing option ⓘ	☐ Request Spot instances	
Network ⓘ	vpc-1a233c78 (10.0.0.0/16) ▾	**C** Create new VPC
Subnet ⓘ	subnet-cc7d01e4(10.0.0.0/24) | us-east-1b ▾ 251 IP Addresses available	Create new subnet
Public IP ⓘ	☑ Automatically assign a public IP address to your instances	

For this example, we created a micro server.

Choose a NAT instance type based on your intended workload. If your application only occasionally needs to connect to the Internet and doesn't require high network bandwidth, then a micro instance will suffice. If your application talks to the Internet continuously and requires better bandwidth, then start with m1.medium instances. You may need to upgrade the NAT instance to m1.large because network I/O varies between instance types.

Now, deselect the "**Source/Destination**" check box, right click on the NAT instance, select "Change Source/Dest. Check", and click on "Disable".

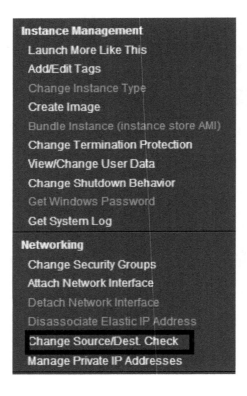

The NAT instance must be able to send and receive traffic from sources or destinations other than itself, so you'll need to deselect the "source/destination" check boxes.

You can find more details <u>here</u>

Now navigate to Security Groups to add rules for inbound traffic.

Go to the Inbound tab for NAT_SG01. These rules will allow app servers to talk to the NAT instance on the 80 and 443 ports.

1. Select "**HTTP**" from the Create a new rule list. In the Source box, specify the IP address range of your private subnet (App server subnets) and then click "Add Rule".

2. Select "**HTTPS**" from the Create a new rule list. In the Source box, specify the IP address range of your private subnet, and then click "Add Rule". Click "**Apply Rule Changes**".

Now navigate to Route Tables and select the private subnets 10.0.1.0/24 and 10.0.2.0/24.

On the Routes tab, specify 0.0.0.0/0 in the Destination box, specify the instance ID of the NAT instance in the Target box, and then click "**Add**".

If you don't need an additional instance for NAT, you can minimize cost by assigning a public IP to the instance that needs Internet access. That will allow the instance to access the Internet directly.

Create App Servers

Now go to Services->EC2 ->Launch Instance.

On the Configure Instance Details page, from the Network list choose the VPC that you created previously and select your app server subnet (10.0.1.0/24, 10.0.2.0/24) from the Subnet list.

Optional: Select the "**Public IP**" check box to request that your app instance receive a public IP address. This is required when you don't have a NAT instance, but your instance requires Internet access.

On the Configure Security Group page, select the option "Select an existing security group" and then select the APP_SG01 security group that you created previously. Click "Review and Launch".

Now log in to the server and check to see whether or not you can access the Internet.

```
$ ping google.com
```

You now might ask, "How can I access from my desktop an instance that was created in a private subnet and has no assigned public IP?" The answer is that you can't. To do so, you'll need a bastion box in the public subnet. You can use a NAT instance as a bastion server (also known as a jump box).

Log in to the bastion (NAT) server first. You can access any instance from this server that was created in a private subnet.

Create RDS

Navigate to Services->RDS

Go to Subnet Groups in the navigation pane and click "**Create DB Subnet Group**".

Select the VPC ID from the drop down menu.

Select "**Availability Zone**" and choose the Subnet IDs of 10.0.11.0/24 and 10.0.12.0/24. Then click "**Add**"

Click "**Yes, Create**" to create the subnet group.

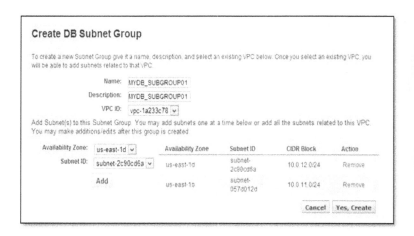

Creating an Options Group and a Parameters Group is similar to doing so in classic EC2.

Launch an RDS instance within the subnet group created above.

In the Additional Config window, select the VPC and DB Subnet Groups created previously.

To make sure that your RDS instance is launched in subnets 10.0.11.0/24 and 10.0.12.0/24, select the "mydb-subgroup01" subnet group.

All other steps for creating an RDS are as usual.

Create ELB

Now it's time to create the amazon load balancer. The load balancer will be the frontend and will be accessible from the Internet, which means that the ELB will be launched in public subnets 10.0.51.0/24 and 10.0.52.0/24.

At this point the two subnets can't access the Internet. To make them public subnets, update the route table that these subnets are associated to.

Navigate to Services->VPC->Route Tables

Select the ELB route table.

On the Routes tab, specify 0.0.0.0/0 in the Destination box, select the Internet gateway in the Target box, and then click "Add".

Navigate to Services-> EC2-> Load Balancers

Click "**Create Load Balancer**".

In the Launch Wizard, select "Create LB inside" as your VPC ID.

Do not select "**Create an internal load balancer**".

Click "**Continue**"

In Add EC2 Instances select the subnets where you want the load balanced instances to be. Select 10.0.51.0/24 and 10.0.52.0/24.

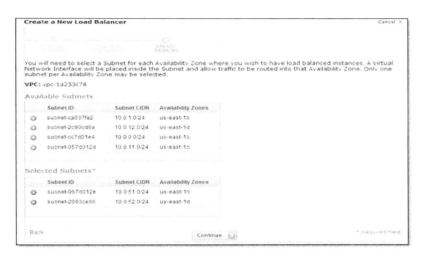

In the next window select "Choose from your existing security group" and then select the ELB_SG01 security group that you created previously. Click "**Continue**".

In the next window select the App servers. Click "**Continue**".

Review the details and click "**Create**".

Make sure that you've enabled the APP_SG01 inbound ports (80/443) to ELB_SG01 so that the ELB can route traffic to backend app servers. Also make sure that ELB_SG01 HTTP and HTTPS ports are publicly accessible (0.0.0.0/0).